What'll We Do with This Life?

What'll We Do with This Life?

Selected Poems by Karl Krolow, 1950–1990

Translated by
Stuart Friebert

Rutherford • Madison • Teaneck
Fairleigh Dickinson University Press
London and Toronto: Associated University Presses

© 1993 by Associated University Presses, Inc.

All rights reserved. Authorization to photocopy items for internal or personal use, or the internal or personal use of specific clients, is granted by the copyright owner, provided that a base fee of $10.00, plus eight cents per page, per copy is paid directly to the Copyright Clearance Center, 27 Congress Street, Salem, Massachusetts 01970. [0-8386-3509-1/93 $10.00 + 8¢ pp, pc.]

Associated University Presses
440 Forsgate Drive
Cranbury, NJ 08512

Associated University Presses
25 Sicilian Avenue
London WC1A 2QH, England

Associated University Presses
P.O. Box 338, Port Credit
Mississauga, Ontario
Canada L5G 4L8

The paper used in this publication meets the requirements
of the American National Standard for Permanence of Paper
for Printed Library Materials Z39.48-1984.

Library of Congress Cataloging-in-Publication Data

Krolow, Karl.
    What'll we do with this life? : selected poems by Karl Krolow, 1950–1990 / translated by Stuart Friebert.
      p. cm.
   ISBN 0-8386-3509-1 (alk. paper)
    1. Krolow, Karl—Translations, English. I. Friebert, Stuart, 1931– . II. Title.
PT2621.R695A244   1993
831'.914—dc20   92-54881
                                                                                    CIP

PRINTED IN THE UNITED STATES OF AMERICA

For the Krolows

Contents

Acknowledgments	11
Introduction	
WALTER HELMUT FRITZ	13

Part One: Someone Says Yes, *but Not for You*

Night	33
The World's Making Something of Itself	34
Shadow Spots	35
The Details Get Lost	36
Restlessness	37
Seasons	38
Life Depends on It	39
Air	40
Trundling Hoops	41
Colors	42
I Myself	43
Sundays	44
The Park	45
Interim	46
In Peace-Time	47
Rustic	49
Old Enough	50
Made Flesh	51
Poem for Literature	52
Simple and Clear	53
Nice	54
Departure	55
Earlier, I	56
Some Time	57

Earlier, II	58
Have You Noticed?	59

Part Two: Someone's Sneaking Off

Between Past Life and the Future	63
Let Live	64
Considering a Landscape	66
There's the Spring	67
Some Countries	68
People on the Move	69
In the Country	70
Old People's Spring	71
Terror	72
Miniature	73
Artist	74
On Biographies	75
In Flight	76
Next Door	77
Reflections	78
Träumerei	79
What There Was	80
Day in Germany	81
These Old Men	82
Parade	83
News of Death	84
July and August	87
Landscape after My Heart	88
At Daybreak	90
Unprepared	91
Family Table	92

Part Three: Someone Who Was Up for Anything

Universal Poem	95
Course of a Day	96
Rain	97
Lullaby	98
Entirely Self-evidently	99

Stranger's Hand in Your Pocket	100
The End of Some Things	101
Don't Think	102
The Other Side	103
The Order of Things	104
Fingers	105
Death as Snowman	106
The Murderer	107
Air-conditioning	108
Cicada	109
Motives	110
Some Things	113
When It Was Time	114
All the Same	115
A Feeble Affair	116
The Year	117
Life	118
The House That Holds Everything	119
Staying Alive	120
Years upon Years	121
The Skin You're Stuck In	122

Acknowledgments

Some of these poems have appeared, sometimes in slightly different form, in the following journals:

American Poetry Review
Artful Dodge
Boston Literary Review
Chaminade Literary Review
Chelsea
Colorado Review
Field
Great Stream Review
Interim
Iowa Review
International Poetry Review
Montana Review
Nebraska Review
North Dakota Quarterly
Ohio Review
Parnassus
Ploughshares
Pennsylvania Review
Quarry West
Salmon Magazine
St. Monica Review
The Poetry Miscellany
Whiskey Island

Introduction

Walter Helmut Fritz

German poetry since 1945 is unthinkable without the effects that emanate from Karl Krolow's works. What Krolow has done is conclusive, and of exemplary import. Hugo Friedrich writes, in his careful, exact essay that accompanies Krolow's *Selected Poems* (1962), that with respect to the later poems, one can claim the best that can be said of a poetic language: "that it is unmistakable." And he speaks—above all, in reference to Krolow's *Foreign Bodies* (1959)—of a mastery that says the unusual in a natural way. He calls the book "a record of modern poetry writing, an important poetic diagnosis of the modern soul." To see this in the proper perspective, one must realize that this is being said by a scholar who is not after highlights, but is rather simply clarifying his findings. Friedrich sees Krolow in a line with Baudelaire, Mallarmé, and Guillèn, treating as he does the proximity of poetic and mathematical vision that is characteristic of modern poetry as a whole.

He calls Krolow's poetry—to stay with his analysis for a moment—a poetry not of feeling but of the imaginative eye, of a combinative inventiveness stemming from flashes of language that trace unknown, galvanic fields in words. The tension between linguistic determination and freedom of content, between objectivity and fictitiousness, between metric precision and syntactic dissolution in the stanzaic poems; the possibility of a logic of the absurd; the technique of forking the meaning of a word into the obvious as well as the irreal at the same time; melancholy objectified to the point of impersonal disillusionment; the creation of irrealities from bits of reality; the artifice of contracting that which has been objectively or spatially widely separated; the lyrical anecdote as brief, unreal, ghostly incident; silence as main theme; the disguise or absence of the speaking I; the predominance of collective labels, body fragments or remains of what is human; the meaning of metaphor; the establishment of a boundary between image and thing; the changes in syntax that lead to the ellipses and shorthand that characterize this poetry; the quiet process to which the syntactical fragments surrender—all this Friedrich demonstrates through elucidating example.

Krolow's poems permit agreement, are open, a kind of regards. He's been called, more often than not, a virtuoso. There's justice in that, but it leads to mistaken notions, if, at the same time, one overlooks the inner assumptions that his kind of virtuosity possesses. His poems are impulses of the attempt to keep life alive—through poems. That's increasingly clear with each volume.

Compared to the poems in *Foreign Bodies,* the poems of *Invisible Hands* (1962) are more laconic. The way the poems end makes that especially clear. "Let's move on, / as long as we can still hear / the blood singing in our ears," in one poem. Or: "The end will come / while paging through pictures, / no one wants / to see anymore." Or: "The baggage of love / is quickly lost." Or: "Under the earth / the dead die once more."

Knowledge of being threatened enters the word, a condition that derives from connections that are at first inconspicuous: "Who will dare talk / of the sharpness / of scythes?" Incredible, the following stanza: "Silence / is the cancer of laughter / during which meals / end faster and faster." That's as frightening and correct an insight as it is convincing in its imagery.

Existence, therefore, that seeks expression; that is conscious of its decrepitude; that has moments of happiness in the poem; that senses how limited the zone is for the possibility of life. "Attempts, / at sustaining breath / which flickers /

like a candle." Bound up here is the attentiveness that promotes life. "Notice everything along the way: / Between going and coming back / snow will fall." Quiet, knowing lines.

But for all the melancholy in these poems there is also, at the same time—sometimes so frankly joyful—a turning toward notions that the meeting of world and imagination calls forth. This poetry is also the result of a specially trained "curiosity." The poem with this title begins: "The supply of eyes / never suffices." Those are two characterizing lines. In addition, Krolow's poems are occasionally journeys "Into the interior moments." That is where the triumphs of the imagination come from; the wind coming over mimosa trees in sleep; morning with its blue eye, astonished at the illegible writing of a breeze on the swimming pond; women with fiery spices in their eyes that set fire to the stacks of grain; the landscape crackling like colored paper someone has lit; September with its raised eyebrow that tires at the sight of migratory birds; little girls selling their braids for a kiss; in a foggy landscape, streets and trees playing blind man's bluff; drinkers falling through the open night with their souls.

Krolow's poems often consist of a hovering transparency. The following piece is called "Sky":

> Arena of sillouhettes!
> They're fighting over
> becoming
> snowflakes or larks.
>
> Summer lets longing,
> blue ships sail through it.
>
> On their journey to the zenith
> they grow lighter and lighter.
>
> Horizon's angels
> waiting for light
> under their eyelashes.

At the same time, one has to remain conscious of the darkness from which such poems come. There is mention in one of "the reliability of the dark." The cold spreads out. "Words freeze in the mouth." Light finds itself in a "crisis." One finds "News of death": "Slow death of the eyes / which no one looks into anymore." And, in the last piece in the collection, Krolow talks of writing paper as of a garland, "withering around the presence of death."

In 1965, Krolow's *Collected Poems* appeared. The appearance of this volume, the first comprehensive collection of his work, will go down in history as an important date in German poetry. About 270 poems in a period of twenty years. Again, it became clear that Krolow's poetry contains patterns by which it is possible to discover reality; that it is able to loosen numbness, decompose functionalism; that disillusion, almost objectified, almost anonymous, drives the stanzas; that we're dealing with versifications of a process of perceiving, a way of understanding; that these poems scan the image we make of the world in order to meet those levels of reality, behind our current classifications, which the more they expose themselves to our observing eye, the more they disguise themselves. These poems have an informative character, of a hard won, hopeful life. Poetry as a secret among people. Poetry that makes one hear more acutely.

What occupied our attention while reading the volume *Landscapes For Me,* that appeared a year later, was the imperturbability which Krolow won from his heightened inner situation. A situation that is somewhat perceptible in a few lines of the poem, "Words in Winter": "Words take refuge in each other / before numbness." Or: "Sometimes / a sentence takes shape, / which doesn't freeze / on the lips." In "Sometimes," one can feel the difficulty of poetic existence, but also the tirelessness with which Krolow keeps on asking questions. One must keep in mind the self-radicalizing situation in order to understand fully how resolute it is.

It is no accident that the poems that concern winter and wintry existence are presented together in a special section of the book. Winter appears as "buried time." It falls like a dead blackbird to the ground. "Conversations are held / without people," according to one poem. Or: "Fingers are / forgotten in gloves." And about words: "Patiently one speaks them / into the cold." That notion of words, spoken patiently into the cold, that sometimes become sentences, that don't freeze on the lips, contains a "summation" of what Krolow "transmits" in this book.

To be sure, brightness and lightness are also involved. One reads of the colloquial language of light clothes, or of every hand, in high summer, waiting for a glass of water. The seventh section of the book brings together a series of pieces that work like a cycle, and differ superficially from the others in the book in that they occasionally appear as one piece, not divided into stanzas like most of the others in the collection, which affords a permeating, apparently casual voice that won't be interrupted. One quickly notes the beginnings, for instance: "Slowly, slowly." Or: "Effortlessly, / just like that, thoughtlessly / this and that—." Or: "Accept it. / Just / let me try it—." Poems of life's moments, in which concentration and flight are one.

The poems, in which Krolow turns to the times of day, and seasons, appear now in greater numbers, focussed from a given distance, by way of a reflecting consciousness that allows things, in ever sharper outline, hence more clearly, to turn into elements of a "dream" that keeps affecting us. The titles are also characteristic in this connection, for instance: "Cartestian May," "Copper Engraving of Autumn," or "Tools for the Light."

Sometimes, Krolow's poems become small "stories." The poem, "Tragedy," is such an example. It ends:

> Let's go
> in the shade of a hat
> eat ice cream!
> Its flavor will put an end
> to the helplessness of feeling.

Lines, in which among other things, we notice the intertwining of horror and gesture that is almost thrown away, that Krolow is able to manage.

In the volumes that follow, *Everyday Poems* (1968), *Nothing More Than Life* (1970), and *Time Passing* (1972)—the poems were reprinted, with more than fifty new ones, in *Collected Poems II*, that apepared in 1975 for Krolow's sixtieth birthday—there is something disturbing that was noticeable before, here and there, but is now clear on a broader base—the stronger inclination to the "everyday," the apparently incidental. The stanzas become simpler, more monosyllabic and laconic, prefer banal, entirely subjective themes, take on a new intensity from this larger voicelessness.

The desire to observe things before they become invisible, magnifies; the desire to have another look at what once was. It is immediately apparent that in two lines like, "The surfaces are / clear to see once more," seeing surfaces again is understood as a developed, late state of happiness. "Growing Older" is the title of a cycle, to which the lines cited above lead. Growing older with "lighter sleep" and this experience:

> A strange mouth
> that robs me of language.
> Listening patiently
> while it names my name.

In this connection, consider some lines from another poem: "Learning to use his language / as a foreign one, tuned in / to something else, that / wasn't known till now / that's here and / makes your voice foreign." Such a stanza clearly shows how Krolow distances himself from the metaphorics of his earlier poems, how a more direct way of talking asserts itself that lends the lines additional "freedom."

Bound up with that is an increase in more subdued, darker colors, in refusing gestures in places, of taciturnity: "The cold. It makes / no words." Another poem ("Getting Snowed In") begins with the words that create stillness: "Farther and deeper." Its ending: "Don't turn around— let no one find / the snow / on our eyes." Pale, wintry light that spreads out, empties the landscape, lets it grow familiar.

Again and again, a barely controlled uneasiness is perceptible that extends to the most significant events:

> I go across the street.
> That doesn't alter the place,
> whether or not I count my steps
> or don't watch out and forget,
> along the way, where I want to go.

Sentences can go in unexpected directions, "idioms get stuck," the darkness is seen as "a change between the lines," borders come closer, but "once more we take a look / at life, before it leaves us." Writing appears as an attempt to gain clarity about whether or not we're really here. The beginning of the last poem goes: "I try / to assure myself / that I occur."

A long way, then, from Krolow's early poems, in part schooled in Loerke's and Lehmann's nature-magical, rhymed poems intent on metaphor, works from an earlier era that are often viewed in relation to French and Spanish poems, on to the late verse, often as if half-voiced. A reference to Krolow's translations is therefore necessary in this respect, because the authors he translated were, in part, important for his own work.

For example, Krolow published, in 1962, his translations into German of *Spanish Poems of the Twentieth Century*. We know how indispensable such a book is; everyone interested in the subject was waiting for it. Because, for one, Krolow possesses intimate knowledge of the subject and the sensitivity that enables him to translate exactly, while at the same time affording him, vis-à-vis the originals, his own fullness of expression in his opposing, heightened German poems; and for another, it's precisely the Spanish poetry of this century—in contrast, say, to French and Italian—that is comparatively little known in Germany. Till then, Krolow had mostly translated from the French. As early as 1948, his *After-Poems of Five Centuries of French Poetry* appeared; in 1957, *The Bark Fantasy,* in which he presented French poets of our century; and his *Verlaine-Selections* appeared the same year and, in 1959, his translations from Apollinaire's *Bestiarium*.

In the intervening years, Krolow also published short prose. There is his *Poetic Journal* (1966). In this volume, he occasionally addresses the stereotypical question often put to writers—why one writes: "One of the countless, unutterable motives that keeps us bent over our typewriter," he finds in an entry in Oskar Loerke's journal: "I can forget my body at times." And Krolow weighs an answer that begins like this: "Come along for a while on my hours and days, and you won't want to repeat [the question], because you'd be more helpless than I, vis-à-vis my subjunctive way of life."

The last sections of the book can be seen in this light. Krolow asks himself for whom he's writing everything. A fool's question, he believes. And: a worried question. Then we read: "For readers, one says. Certainly: For readers. What presumption, to take readers into account." And somewhat farther along, he notes that the writing process is full of egoism and frivolity; which doesn't preclude its being a helpless process, what someone does who can't be advised or helped; who "asks after nothing and no one and by this very behavior suddenly comes into contact with strangers, with people and events far distant." Also instructive is Krolow's observation that he's noticed that he not only writes for people but also for so-called dead objects, for landscapes, times of day, cities, "for sorrow and bodily pain," in order to allow both people and things a more reconciling relationship.

The book contains a series of such fundamental responses to questions about writers' work; the incalculability of the "hand that writes"; the meaning of accidents for the creative process; the often necessary "preparation for passionate, headlong exertion." Krolow talks of how music, playing tapes or records, can heighten one's sensitive attention while working, while hindering the "petrification" of collecting oneself; that writing is an expedition, during which almost nothing happens ("everything's over quickly / like the turn of the head"). There is special notice, again and again, of the poem itself; of lyrical laconicism, say, during which at times "sharp ears heard the noise of teeth grinding." Or, Krolow maintains that he's afraid, in fickle moments; the time of lovely surprises in the poem may be past, because poetry itself had long since become definite, relentless. Or he notes the circumstance in which poems one wrote years ago can seem stranger than someone else's.

Such remarks are often inserted into meditations on times of day and seasons, where Krolow mostly pays attention to certain alternating effects. For example, he mentions that heat, light, and quiet can be exceptionally stimulating while writing, lead to a "jubilation of particulars," produce an intensity "that extends beyond solely bucolic statements." One can well see in all this how close he comes, again and again, to the poem; when he finds sleep going along upright, past his house, drawn by night, coming on; air assuming a sea-blue body in order to approach an unknown woman; death, in a Portuguese cloister, having to penetrate the quiet of the cork of the monks' cells whenever death went to them (lines that point to the poem, "In Portugal").

Once, he talks of translation; of the book-jungle of a family library; of the "memory" of a mirror; of authors who are present in important quotes, for example Fargue with his sentence that death is God's serious toy, or Heinse, whose "Ardinghello" Krolow labels one of the very few examples of important German fiction without metaphysical ambition. Several pages are devoted to Harry Graf Kessler's journal notebooks, in which a visit to Paul Verlaine is described. Verlaine's life-long companion was putting up red currants which apparently disturbed the German visitor. Krolow: "One feels (without sympathy) how hard it is, for the one who would later become Maillol's promoter, to accept the imperturbable charm of this muse of practical reason. Madame knew what she was doing when she went about preserving without fussing over the cosy guest from Germany. . . . The decorum, with which someone was looked after there, still delights after such a long time. It's a book, mentioned once in connection with Wackenroder, that treats the human spirit in its relationship to magic, comfort and discretion." Three key words one can't ignore that are a part of the intimacy of sharing that has grown rare—which one can encounter in these notebooks.

A kind of continuation of this book is the *Minute-Notebooks* (1968). Again Krolow prefers the suddenly shifting point of view. Again, quotations assume special meaning. Sometimes it contains those key words, of which he speaks in one passage: "Writing is dependent upon key words. . . . Key word as darting flame. Without a sound it shoots into a sky of sensitive tension." Sometimes, the quote "sums up" what Krolow previously presented in detail.

At times, there are a few pages of extensive commentary. For instance, on questions of literature—Krolow noting that today we don't have a connection anymore to a literature that is based on the golden mean; that pleasant proportion in the work of art has a repelling or boring effect; that the exemplary is often lifeless, and perfection can turn into puppetry. The fully realized puppet is of a cold fascination, an icy eroticism . . . something that is everywhere "correct . . . a figure that knows no effort and no loss, a thing that is successful for all time, and freezes in its perfection."

Or, he maintains that the writer today comes from a literary means of expression that increasingly tires, that is spoiled by literary convention that has been achieved increasingly hastily; that everyone moves through "a personal odyssey of language learning"; that ironic balance can be effective "when so-called literary truth broaches the embarrassment of its irrefutability and doesn't know what to do with its own certainty anymore. Whenever it had become necessary to point to its knowingness, its arrogance."

Krolow talks of the occasional pathos of quiet language; of how the quiet can also be intrusive, namely when reserve loses its credibility, when it turns into a poetic lisp, a strained whisper. In this connection, he mentions Klopstock (in the chapter, "Writing with Light"), who furnished his odes with a severe light but didn't always just write soft and quiet things. "The aura that surrounds them came to pass at times beneath seraphic rumbling, which has nothing to do with any sort of poetic silence. It is light, as angelic sound, as trumpet call, as flourish, announcing poetic perception. . . . Klopstock's poetry is light-impregnated, without letting light through. It's more a matter of spiritual, intellectual perception, a block melting into its brightness." In observations like these, we can see especially clearly the certainty of vision, the specific clarity, the intellectual and spiritual tension that these notes reveal in many instances.

One finds brief portraits, like this one of Jean Follain: "A spiritual, intellectual, museful peasant from the northern provinces. . . . A sensitive gorilla could look like that. His French, less spoken than snorted, is not easy to understand." One finds impressions of journeys, for instance the four "Little Day- and Night-pieces" that refer to Paris. And again and again meditations on time ("the easy use of time in muscles and faces"), loneliness ("one must cover one's ears for loneliness"), truth ("when it enters, truth is unutterable"), or the "stone of sages, always asleep somewhere under the mortar. Right there, where no one expects it." Krolow talks of the "fixed idea of meeting someone again who no longer exists," of the moment when decades ago a dead girl seemed to be coming toward him from among the people passing by on the street of a big city. "She had new movements, because she'd been dead. . . . She had something that estranged her from me for all time, while slowly approaching and holding her face to the streetlight, as if in greeting, something I couldn't reciprocate."

Occasionally, one encounters observations of body-consciousness. Krolow maintains that there is sufficient opportunity to experience the organism that one otherwise perceives as a unity, as a "desolate region," something that is unsettled and distant, does not belong to one. Contrariwise: "Looking at randomness, I take notice of the laws of my body which tries to assert itself. In this way, the human body, with its firmness of flesh, the reality of its proportions, can become a living treatise against formlessness."

With the notebooks of both volumes, Krolow has realized a possibility of literary speech that—between journal and essay—above all, gives play to the element of reflection and a way of thinking, determined by the imagination. He has collected essays in the classical sense in two other books. His *Aspects of Contemporary German Poetry* (1961) contain— with minor changes—the six lectures he gave at the University of Frankfurt during the winter semester of 1960–61. Poetry other than German poetry is considered only in reference to the political poem. Krolow spoke as a "practitioner." As he notes, in that sense he has always preferred the way of spontaneous expression to that of dealing fundamentally with objects, as is the task of the sciences. Lectures, therefore, from a "realized moment," demonstrating the immediacy of reaction.

"Possibilities of contemporary German poetry" is the title of the first chapter. Fundamentals, hypotheses, the parallelism of many voices, many generations, discussions among single classifications, possibilities of expression, the question of how the German poem could free itself from isolation after 1945, mistrust vis-à-vis oneself and vis-à-vis the poem, sensory escape-adventures from the prison of the self, more and more the case due to one's own refinements, one's engaging the self so fully, and questions, always new questions— all this is sketched in the first pages.

In the second chapter—"Possibilities and limits of the new German nature poetry"—Krolow elucidates "the reduction of the human picture, or image, that runs together with the development of the nature poem." Nature poetry, in general, he takes as a countermovement to the dying, late-expressionism of the 1920s. He interprets poems of Loerke, Lehmann, Elisabeth Langgässer, and Günter Eich, in order to show, by example, the lineage right on to Peter Huchel and Heinz Piontek.

Further sections are devoted to "the structure and character of the modern love poem," to the special problems the love poems faces today, the "deep disturbances," the "increasing distances and estrangements." In this regard, Krolow takes an especially critical look at Gottfried Benn, further, the parablelike language in Brecht and Ingeborg Bachmann,

Eich's laconicism, Helmut Heissenbüttel's case, Hans Magnus Enzensberger's lyric fairy-tale, skeletalizing in Eugen Gomringer, Peter Härtling's lyrical figurine, and the quiet ballet of Paul Celan.

"The political poem as public poem" is the theme of the fourth lecture. The political, Krolow emphasizes, is only a superficial designation. Of political poems in the actual sense of the word, one can perhaps talk of Georg Herwegh's, Hoffmann von Fallersleben's, Ferdinand Freiligrath's, Richard Dehmel's. The newer political poem takes on more general, "public" features, has more of an "institutional" character. It is practiced, above all, in Anglo-Saxon countries. Krolow concerns himself more closely with W. H. Auden, Randall Jarrell, Karl Shapiro, Allen Ginsberg, Robinson Jeffers, but also with Frenchman like Louis Aragon and Paul Eluard.

Additionally, Krolow's attention goes to the "poem as game, or play." He understands the playful as an important factor in the general process of de-individualization, which the poem participates in at the moment, as "an attempt to flee the thicket of meanings, the impenetrable jungle of poetic individuality, that threatens to smother itself." He demonstrates this extensively in Hans Arp and indicates it in Günter Grass.

In the middle of the last chapter—"speechlessness, silence, and emptiness in the contemporary German poem"—there is Paul Celan. But the highly calculated language of Helmut Heissenbüttel also is examined as well. And finally, Krolow turns to the more recent experimental poetry.

These lectures are distinguished by their exact sense of subject matter; by Krolow's ability to clarify the abundance of subject matter, to show lines, or "aspects,"; by the liveliness of the formulations; by a sensitivity and sensibility that has tested itself over many years in the construction of his own poetic world.

Similar things obtain in *Shadow-Skirmishes* (1964). The piece that lends the book its title is a conversation between A. and B., about the poem and the one who writes it. It offers a concentrate of insight into the difficulties of the matter under discussion. It shows in particular, Krolow's own position, but at the same time points so fully to fundamentals that it can only be understood as a dialogue about the situation of the contemporary poem in general.

At one point, we read: "I don't like any ballast. Along the way I always wanted less consumption, less expense, because I had to keep going. At least I talked myself into it, and by giving myself this kind of courage, something came of it again: one line, two lines, a poem. In this way, I left poems behind." This is said after decades of work, relentless reflection, countless "skirmishes," a restlessness that seldom let up, when one notices "how in the poems it grows quieter and quieter, how less and less is realized from them, how the meanings get away." The ascertained fact is conclusive for Krolow's poem, and it proves true—aside from all the differences—for the contemporary poem as well, growing more lonely everywhere where it is not silenced by slogans, where its existence, its essence, its form and structure are not hidden by placards.

In the other pieces in the book, Krolow deals with separate literary subjects. In the essay, "Lyric and Landscape," he offers a view of the development of the landscape poem from the eighteenth century to the present. He shows how lyric and landscape join for the first time (and for a long time, for the only time) in a connected sense that still obtains in the work of Salis-Seewis; how this poet succeeds in letting landscape become independent of the imparting individuality of the poet; how, in his work, it knows none of the disturbances to which the landscape of classic and Romantic poetry were exposed; how the German landscape poem of the nineteenth century recovered only gradually from such "disturbances"; how Droste-Hülshoff's landscape poetry grows visible in its lonely stature, in an exactitude not previously known, without any pretext; how landscape in Stefan George can become static, occasionally statesque, "a provoking relapse"; how in Georg Heym, Ernst Stadler, Georg Trakl, the "forced" landscapes of expressionism, in Gottfried Benn the verbal violence become clear; how the "wherewithal of the human from the overseen landscape" proceeds in some of Däubler's pieces, but especially in Loerke and Lehmann; how in Langgässer, the economy starts breaking up here and there; how Piontek realizes a new, blurred contour, no longer possessed by too strong a sense of detail, and how in Eich's and Rainer Brambach's landscape poems, people show up again.

Another piece concerns the role of the author in the experimental poem, the question of to what extent individuality—as seen in the development in poetry—is permitted in the lyrical text. Krolow demonstrates the process of de-individualizing in examples, for instance in Langgässer, in whose work rank detail overpowers itself; in Celan, where the tendency to dilute objectivity, to shadow, is characteristic; in E. E. Cummings, who takes full advantage of gestured and typographical stimuli; in Heissenbüttel, where the language —grammatically meditative throughout—is self-referential. Krolow not only documents processes, but also—in other, less self-sufficient authors—points up characteristic hypertropes, "word-swell," and "naked word-catalogues." And he writes: "The consequences of the thorough retreat of the problematic individuality of the author from the poem are clear enough. Terror, in literature, is also the consequence of a certain methodology. The horror that the text that is left to itself exudes attests to the whole critical state of the development that modern textualization has assumed." Important, too, the essay of the poet-translator of contemporary poetry. Krolow not only talks of hypotheses for the understanding of the problem: of "the hardening process," of "incest" before 1945, the oversupply of names, powers, impulses in the fifties, the ever faster shrinking of distances among national literatures, the resulting, enhanced possibilities for understanding, but also of the danger of monotony that grows evident at times. He clarifies—by using one of Apollonaire's animal poems that he translated—specific difficulties that arise during translation, above all from the French. He emphasizes that it is especially a matter of establishing a related climate, and suggests that there is no canon of behavior; that one must always begin again if one wants to ascertain the foreign voice.

And finally, Krolow provides an overview of the laconic in modern poetry, characterizing it as a purifying element, as a possibility for hardening poetry, tightening it, by the addition of prose structures. He follows the development in America (Whitman, Williams, Cummings, Creely, Ferlinghetti), points out the differing forms in France, the nightmarish in Michaux, Guillevic's circumspection, and, in conclusion, draws a picture of the situation in Germany, where Brecht went the farthest with the laconic mode, where later additions result, the magic in Eich, the fantastical-scurrilous in Dieter Hoffmann. This too is a piece, in which—by way of examples—a deeply fundamental process is fully clarified. A rich volume, governed by a self-possessed passion for the business of poetry, which shows lines and at the same time an abundance of subject matter, written out of great inner tension, "objective," and yet very much Karl Krolow in every single sentence.

Krolow's most recent collection, *Ich höre mich sagen* (*I hear myself say*, 1992), while still insistent upon the life-long qualities discussed above, manages to reach as well for something slightly more personal, warmer in tone, more vulnerable, not so detached, as if he had caught himself saying things with his whole being that only part of him had said or heard before. One thinks of a few other great European contemporaries, Miroslav Holub or Italo Calvino, say, who while still serving ideals like quickness, lightness, exactitude, visibility, and multiplicity (see Calvino's *Six Memos for the Next Millennium*, 1988), now hold out for a sixth, something like loyalty to self.

—Translated by Stuart Friebert

What'll We Do with This Life?

One

Someone Says *Yes*, But Not for You

NIGHT

No debates or arguments—
you can feel your Adam's apple growing,
surely an error, because
it's so cold, body to body.
Finally, you call people up
if there's a telephone around.
Someone says YES, but not for you.
And: I won't leave you.
You taste blood on your tongue,
as in some stories
others have told.
Sleep will make me
even older.

THE WORLD'S MAKING SOMETHING OF ITSELF

Friends, the world's making something of itself.
The air's a simplified aria.
The astonishingly polluted air's
not transitional, as earlier.
I know, we have time.
You can go here and there.
There are no hostile noises.
The air's a microphone
the wind talks into, shyly.
I'd really like
to observe your toes
when you're naked
or see strawberries before me
on a white plate.
They're being harvested somewhere right now,
once and for all on this
summery earth.

SHADOW SPOTS

The carnation doesn't know the carnation.
Summer's a high fever.
In the brief shadows
you can see the spine of things.
The landscape agreeing,
A trace of blood, drying:
July.
You light what wants to burn—
Grass patterns, formed from short grass.
Life derives from carbon.
Shadow spots roam
over the table
you fall asleep at.

THE DETAILS GET LOST

In the evening. I read stories
for the night that lacks will
at one corner of the table.
I don't burn holes
in the tablecloth or
the skin of porcelain.
I've got the feeling
I don't belong in my clothes.
Her hair's a part of the darkness.
She loves me so.
Newspaper rustles differently.
I know the way we write
proper names can change
while we occupy ourselves
powerlessly with our bodies.
The details
gradually get lost.

RESTLESSNESS

Childhood and youth
of roads that run through the land
and make places with blossoming trees
restless.
A time of the usual urges—
love that
won't wait,
experienced in the usual
places.
The restlessness continues
when things turn green.
Grass grows slowly
in the cold shadows
before evening comes, moonthirsty
and night falls
like a piece of ice from the sky.

SEASONS

Each spring starts with exaggerations.
How breathless, this rustling. A crayon
grows restless, and a coup d'état appears
out of the blue, the Marseillaise of birds—

a text you can't resist. Everyone knows it
overnight. Earlier, people just sighed,
had more time. Today
everything's quick and green with finality.

Afterward, a quiet sort of roaring: summer.
Gone the fake princess, the bitter black alder.
All that's been poeticized. But now
each of us must guard against thirst
the best he can. And Trakl's fall commences.

LIFE DEPENDS ON IT

Better:
to read music
than the truth about yourself,
which can't be found anywhere anyway.
It's a matter of
pasting the right stamp
on the letter
and listing
no one's return address
or God's and the world's.
The voice of love's
long since gone out
in the telephone.
Hang back, with
your goods and chattels.
You'll displease
if you catch someone's eye.
There are
more dangerous diseases
than the flu,
for example:
carrying your head high.
The end of that
novel's inconspicuously
deadly.

AIR

I made myself some air every which way.
It remained nicely invisible.
No one saw me petting it.
We went on living together. I felt great
standing there
Finding what I sought in the air.
I was partial to it because
it was all around me.
And it stood by me when I
breathed differently or lost
my temper and tried to grab it
with my arms or grew
timid in my career.

How ravishing the imagination!
Can't say anything against the lucky ones.
I'm lucky. I sense
no one'll bother me
if I keep doing nothing
but write in the air.

TRUNDLING HOOPS

Children, trundling their hoops—
that's fallen out of fashion. Jumping
out of windows, on the other hand, continues
to be in vogue. Though we don't like to talk about
the plunge that's gone on too long, then
the splat. Indeed, we look away.
Don't even listen. For most of us
free fall's much too successful
for living on.
Before you've drunk up,
you choke on your horror.
That's bad for you. The future
was simply interrupted too suddenly.
How wonderful it was, way back when,
watching those hoops down unused roads.
We almost joined in.

COLORS

Sleepwalking colors.

The red of a cheek remembers
the red of tile.

A lightbeam turns into
the exotic drawing
of the moment.

Secret love of horizon-blue
for a girl's blue veins.

A lonely man
scribbles his shadow
at her feet.

Every yellow knows the story
of a lemon.

I MYSELF

I can't see what there was before me.
In the distance, an exchange of words is going on
while I notice how my
left hand falls asleep,
a sort of release.
Passing time the usual way's
not for me—soccer games
on the transistor, cards, billiards.
There's no panorama of life
to see through thick leaves.
Something's over with. I'm not
so surprised anymore
when someone passes by
with a glib hello.
I'm putting an end to inventions.
It's my uncertain profession now
to wait things out, not to
trumpet my feelings.
Do that and life's pleasant.
I'm quite simply just myself now.

SUNDAYS

Sundays, it's not any different either.
A faucet drips into the pail
at the wall of a house, neglected windows
left open, their curtains blowing,
a quiet hum, from where you don't know,
the distant turnpike.
Birds keep still toward noon.
The telephone rings
in an empty room.
You know why and shun the parallels.
You like seedy things,
what's private in your possession,
like second-hand articles.
You feel safe
in unsafe situations,
their mechanics, and don't
take pains to
finish your sentences.

THE PARK

In winter the hedges here
wear a beard like
Karl Marx, in the snow.
In the warm rain
you feel his hair grow,
hold your hand out
as if getting
a present.
Nothing's without a reason.
Then, in summer,
carnation blood rises
bright red to their heads.
Visionaries
pick
the hypertonic flowers.
When fall comes—
melancholy woodfires
having long since gone out—
you close your eyes,
soon feel lamplight
under your lids:
the dark's so bright.
Finally, the logic
of seasons gets lost.
You want to go on living,
uncared for: the park
on your mind, there
where your pituitary gland
weighs half a gram.

INTERIM

Winter fell off the roof as snow,
and spring's hesitant, still no leaves
and bare. The prints of dry twigs. Does
anyone still believe it'll be green after

the first warm rain? Nothing's
alive now. Bushes turn in the wind
like dry spindles. There's giddiness
in the air, a swaying to the light

that suddenly falls on what's survived:
roaming dogs, the cry of roosters.
The cat carries the mouse off
in its jaws, while the spindle shivers.

IN PEACE-TIME

I

Peace. The quiet people
let their hair grow.

The careful prose
of their movements.

Sharp air, when a
teenager pisses
in the ruins of a barracks.

My flower blooms
a long long time.

Love thine enemies:
orderly indifference.

Rustic days everywhere,
innocent as hay piles
from the childhood
of Restif de la Bretonne.

No huge bells. Peace.

II

The poorly paid activity
of recognition.

Yes, the city outskirts
with their concrete mixers!

Johnny and his fortune
on a tatooed chest.

The overrun
paratroopers
have been dead a long time.

My friend, the pastry baker:
"Love reminds us
of our good education."

The future that's been computed
has arrived: boredom.

III

Letting yourself go.

Only visible on a stamp
now: the State.

Melancholy makes progress
the mate's short watch
among fish
slowly rotting away.

Small fruits, shaped
like a tumor.

Ellipse's victory
over death.

Vegetating.

RUSTIC

Barns and summery days.
The tree's stiff leaves
burned. I carry the ashes
to the shed. This place

crackles with summer and love,
when the year turns dark.
Old-fashioned apple thieves
haven't been in trouble for years.

There's a photograph that shows
the rustic pictures of yesterday.
In the dark, a Western's flickering,
its murder more tense than ever.

OLD ENOUGH

All sorts of things happen all over
at any one time for the last time.
The first time
was long ago. When we're
old enough and foolish enough
for some, each of us thinks
I've still got a lot going for me,
and run around with
a lot of little goodbyes.
Vocabulary comes easier.
Things that are over with
you never forget enough.
Charming people, I mean
all sorts of different people,
don't notice at all
what's missing:
a big slice of life,
honest love and a lot
of variety, though your arteries
grow narrower.
Here's an aria from the opera:
Passion.
One applies poetic license,
calls it passing ardor.
Later others will say
how you couldn't perform anymore.
That doesn't count at all.
What does, much much more,
is good cheer, in case
you can add some.

MADE FLESH

Made flesh—that gets too
close to you.
Don't sit on my skin,
stubborn as this
adjective, and excessively near:
an opinion, a body,
the next best thing, then
the worst. Something sitting
too deep in the flesh,
a thorn, an outlook
grown large, almost an
ideology by now—eyes
start rolling. You know
better:
suspicion incarnate,
made of flesh, which
you can't get rid of.
The next best thing's
blossoming away,
in vain.
The worst
has already happened.

POEM FOR LITERATURE

With no similarity to living
or dead persons, literature remains
truly romantic for disengaged moments
with giggling-phases in an ordered life.
A large bouquet of roses
is called for now or
let's start with the full moon
shining inconsiderately
on subversives and other people.
Later, things will improve even more
in soliloquies on a public street.
To its advantage, the world shifts
gradually without respectable examples.
You're just able
to jump your own shadow
and wind up wholly alone
as when making love,
you keep going, on and on,
without finding any resistance
in strangers' apartments,
find two, three, oh many opportunities
to lie down with someone or
quite simply break out in tears
as when reading lovely poems.

SIMPLE AND CLEAR

Everywhere there are tons of people
out walking, because it's
Sunday. People take each other
by the hand and
under the skin.
In France, it used to smell
of 'caporal.' Household soap
was part of our nature:
nice afternoons
with soft spots, once—
now with all the noises
you can think of. Deafening,
that quick, American cuss word.
A tame starling rattles it off,
gets raisins for its efforts.
Everyone's got his own speed.
The instruction of illiterates
is growing
on the walls of houses.
Everything's simple and clear,
and communication's
a lonely word.
Some seem shoved
into the clothes of the dead:
intellectuals.
Soccer games
were held a day early.
In the beginning, it broke
many a heart.

NICE

Nice, like repeating
something done with the hand.
At the same time, you exist: deadly
for me, pure and manic.
Nice, like deception
or edible matter
and whatever remains
of disease: deadly.
Nice: palpable in a pathological
way, and eating whatever
you like with your hands.
Nice, like
forgetting winter
every summer: it's
so deadly, like
blood sugar fluctuation,
when you let yourself be possessed,
impure, still quite frigid.
Later, there's soft dust,
painted eyes: nice
like the mouth moving
while talking. I'm
listening now: to a strange grammar.
How do we live?

DEPARTURE

Each time I leave
for the last season
blood rises
in my ears,
occasionally nothing else
occurs but
a tricky title
for something
no longer written.
Besides, who needs to
be anything now but
a traveller going below.
Any given point's
o.k. with you:
you get through arrival
without gaping.
Life's back there with
the last postal date, indistinguishable.
Time for one last lovely song,
one beat of blood, a gurgling:
deceptive as it can be,
no transition to it,
that's it for your calendar.
You still think you can think:
it's enough.

EARLIER, I

when life
left something to be desired
and the great trees
still stood, unprepared
for loss of leaves,
when the soul
still hadn't begun to rustle around
in the refrigerator at night
and time lost its way
on detours,
when God, with that severe upper lip,
spoke from clouds,
and no one asked,
in a pretty place,
"Do you speak German?"
When a sick neighbor
really started dying
next door,
and mother and child looked for
the battered women's shelter in vain—
when everything really was
much much worse,
when the moon rose so magically
—these days we'd shake our head—and
there was no lack of bibles,
death aplenty
waiting patiently
the other side of funerals.
Genetics is contained
is unborn brains.
A break in the brain was a way
of accommodating the unavoidable,
the way life
leaves something to be desired.

SOME TIME

Don't speed up anything by stammering
that will happen anyway.
Better to let yourself be seen beforehand
as someone who still exists,
without an unpleasant death some time
and other things no one likes to talk about.
Turn the light to dark
or leave the room,
I mean move without any strain
as if no one were there.
Sit quietly. You're not disturbing anyone.
A case of love looks quite different.
There are no flowers for living on.
You'll find the right style
to disappear when there's a chance.
No one will call you up:
come back.

EARLIER, II

There were bare fingers
that reached for spider legs,
earlier, earlier, when fingernails
weren't brittle yet,
and I imitated the bird
that no one called by name.
Hold up a second!
You were wearing a very particular dress,
a nodding carnation
in your lips,
earlier, when people said, "love love."
You'd lost your shadow
when you turned unfaithful
and old time suddenly
sounded different.
Other pulses.
It ran down without a shadow.
We were lucky
nothing happened
waiting for
the lightning to tear us apart.

HAVE YOU NOTICED?

You're loquacious.
I see our imaginary life
rushing past: a Morse code.
Heaps of leaves in country corners.
It's fall and you're voluble.

Something new's knocking at the shutters.
Not another word about summer, yellow as straw.
Stubborn birds are on the wing,
and my armpits are cold.

Forget all that. Come closer, can't you.
There's no intimacy
to our words.
Have you noticed this,
then that?
The swallows that dart along so low are gone.
I've got only one face
when you look at me.

Someone's Sneaking Off

BETWEEN PAST LIFE AND THE FUTURE

Well, well, here I am, I say,
on the way with sentences
that respond to the past.
Even objects
have a past life,
while someone lets a piece
of paper fly like a swallow,
producing the present
with its thrilling
levity,
at once the beginning
of a story that's
called the future.
Here I am, I say
with aggressive melancholy.
Well, well, the gas pressure's low
at the moment, and the opportunity
to say goodbye, take your leave,
not especially propitious.

LET LIVE

I

On flagpoles
the red or white weather
of governments reigns.
I go walking along
underneath, my eyes open.

Above me, in a sky
that's respectful, it blooms
like geraniums today.

They're allowing my neck
and knees to live.
My wrists are
unmolested too.

The hangman's hens
go on taking their bath
in the colorless sand.
The air, like ferns,
grew sensitive.

Sometimes I write in a letter
that my head knows some things perfectly well
and nods politely.

II

The dining tables are
cleared without any noise.

The air everywhere's
blue as a jay's egg:
air for cheerful
delegates.

Who'd like to breathe it
free of charge?
My left hand's
the partner of
my right hand.

It's not only children who love
the pink of paper snakes.
My right and left eye,
equally entitled,
can watch the bronze beasts
lying in front of public buildings,
more and more helpless in
sun that's on the increase.

CONSIDERING A LANDSCAPE

This landscape, like
a national anthem.

Its beard in the wind: much too green.
Too old
for the birds that
mate in it.

Add a sky
with soft soles,
poem-sky,
huge opening of eyes.

Everywhere the green paint.
It colors the fingers
and false notes.

The national air
rises in the air.

THERE'S THE SPRING

There's the spring
of Botticelli
with its known attributes—
a difficult time
for virgins.

The corners of houses stink
of rotting hyacinth bulbs.

SOME COUNTRIES

Some countries are made of earth.
Some we only know from books.
Here you can walk nicely through the air.
There you sit on vegetables,
deal in provisions.
France comes along with an odor
of women's clothes.
England's gray flannel and
very early exploitation.
But in Spain Thousand-and-one's
in Mozart's catalogue of arias.
In some countries gold's the issue,
which is dug for.
Some countries get by on hygiene.
I'm not thinking of America.
Some are private like a secret kiss.
You have to hunt for them
on the map.
Some countries need logic.
Others smell
of chestnuts and walnuts,
and in many, in bad times,
children and customs are
ruder than usual.
Some countries don't exist at all.
They're the hope
of all other lands.

PEOPLE ON THE MOVE

The ones who do see some things.
A cloud beautifies the sky.
There's smoke over a chimney.
I went off, got in my own way.

Meanwhile, stories come to me
about human contradiction or
the climbing of ladders. You can
anticipate the fall.

It happens as simply as possible.
People moving see it differently.
The pleasure of life bounds by,
distant as a river that's
hidden by a landscape.

Some things spread their own news.
As simply as possible, and
one thing just lives off the next,
or some things just call themselves off.
One region stops altogether, greatly amused.

People on the go see more—
ghosts, say, with natural eyes.
This happened, or that did.
From far off there's music!
People drifting go toward it, or away.
Forget themselves. Are already forgotten.

IN THE COUNTRY

In the country the houses
smell
of overheated lime
and the loneliness
of objects.
A chair's nothing
but a chair,
a scissors a scissors, open
or closed.
Slowly it cuts
paper or flesh
that turns red.
Blood's a healthy
color.
The tools used
to kill hang
calmly on the wall:
hammers, pliers.
A gun gets into
your hand easily.
Shoot and hit
the white of the lime,
the white of the eye
of the wall.

OLD PEOPLE'S SPRING

Spring. Elements
of repetition.
There are various
scenes. A curtain's
drawn aside.
Everyone sees what's next:
green, yellow,
the arrangement
of individual colors
on a stage.
A hesitant theater.
The audience consists
of old people
breathing deeply.

TERROR

Truth, if it wants to shine,
needs terror.
People trust blood
that leaves the body,
trust revolution, the courageous
act of violence that cozies
up to power as everyone's
affair—everyone who
dispatches matters
artfully and goes about
it seriously,
overlooking no one vis-á-vis
the truth that looks
back with burning eyes.
The coarseness of an act
filled with devotion.
There's no spot, no town
where the world's
at an end.

MINIATURE

In a small picture
the blue sky's also
small
with its tiny bit of air
above all,
small proportions and
a plot of land
cut just right for
trees, people and pets,
arranged by an unknown
intelligence
that remained outside
the picture, considering
the frame in which
it placed
small things.

ARTIST

He doesn't cut off an ear,
or nail it to the wall.
A bucket of black tea's
enough to make him thirsty for
a simple way of writing.
A bug flying headlong
into its misfortune, humming,
suffices: the halogen light
warming the backs of his hands
and the tiny prose
of a few sentences.
He knows: an unknown master's
happy with a spot of blood
on the sleeve of his jacket,
foreseeing every murder.
A fixed idea
chains him like everything
that's transitory.
Feeling possessed was his
standard attempt not to
deceive himself about good fortune.

ON BIOGRAPHIES

It's good to die young
for biography. We see dead
poets as swans for a while.
They're fed, not made of synthetic material.

Our pretty streets fill up again with folks.
No one thinks about the end of something. That's just
   fine.
A character puts on some dust, a sensitive process.
There's gushiness in the air. Say, how're you living?

No one notices me going about. I try,
I get embarrassed. I've missed a chance
at metamorphosis. I'm still around, incidentally.
I live very well on the deception of my senses.

I won't be fed. The swan's costume's
too old, you can't find faith anymore
at the edge of Swan Lake, and Tschaikowsky's
out of fashion now. Biography's too long.

IN FLIGHT

Poplars, embankments,
the Loire behind them.
The upper Danube's not so
broad, from river to river
the light's so different.
One doesn't need geography
for feelings. Birds fly
up the branches. Watch
us. Feelings are vulnerable.
Strange bodies rub
together, our bodies.
Someone plants a kiss
between navel and shame.
A doorknob turns
on a strange door.
We enter.
Later I looked
for a scissors,
cut out pictures of women.
I didn't find yours.
The poplars, the Loire—
a helicopter above.
Looking for me,
in flight from my feelings,
a waltz by Brahms
from an open window.
He was sitting in a chair,
looking at my flight, staring:
life, beyond recall,
came back.

NEXT DOOR

They're dancing next door. Kiss me. I'm freezing.
It's so dark, and as for women
in old-fashioned nightgowns—
you only see their toes.

They're talking loud next door. Be soft with me.
That's the start of something else.
It's night, and plants
with Latin names smell good.

They're silent next door. I'm afraid.
A water pipe's making noise next door.
They're washing in old-fashioned ways
before they make love.

You can hear the scream next door.
It lasts and lasts. Kiss me.
Someone dies next door: it sounds
quite beautiful. I'd like to die.

REFLECTIONS

A dangling rope's looked at attentively.
And thinking of knives is a good thing;
we put off what we can do.
It's nice not doing anything at all.
We never seem to notice a journey of lovers.
The upper lip's covered with fuzzy hair,
the knotted rope's well hidden.
We notice nothing. We just make some quiet tracks,
test this and that; and physically we're
still there, our mouth dry, licking
at our beard stubble, considering death, thinking we're
  wise.

TRÄUMEREI

Sometimes I get dizzy
watching rushing water.
Robert Schumann
would understand.
I've known some who've
disappeared in water.
I'm water-shy
and avoid the word
for a wet death.
A bit of a compulsion to wash
comes to my rescue.
I can't wash my hands
often enough.
That's enough.
There's that suspicious
roaring again.
The flooding of the eyes
is a mild sort of drowning.

WHAT THERE WAS

There was justice
and physical education,
gymnastics too, and time itself,
minus turbidity.

There was morality.
A woman went past:
the inexorable
in the form of fillips.

There were other things and
the misunderstanding known as love,
that quick, ready mouth,
those delicate thieves of the soul,

was truth, was treason
in all their friendliness,
the Republic, the State.
Time kept slipping away.

There was even recognition.
Which makes it hard for everyone.
The mere naming of names
will turn up none we like.

DAY IN GERMANY

Day of blue fingernails,
with German eyes, nothing
for friends of logarithms.

At the well, leafgreen's
washed till it's white:
dust from feelings you
can write with, for example:
Gothic or with guns.

Wine at the table:
it makes the drinkers dark.
They fall right through
the open night with their souls.

THESE OLD MEN

These old men no one
looks at anymore, pedlars with imagination,
real zeros, repealing their lives,
waiting under trees in the park
for nothing but the past—
a map of dust.
Hidden sentences live on in them
in their dry mouths.
Some have a nice face
for a moment or two. Almost no bodies,
people say. Who knows anything
about these small figures,
moving away?

PARADE

It depends on the dust
the frozen water
doesn't chase away.

The riders are always
just a little ahead of their horses.

Minutes speak
with many feet.

Even the world
of guns traveling by
is an attempt
to bring down roses.

On the balcony the chessplayers
are just another instance
of force.

They lift their heads
when the last soldier
dissolves
in the sudden rain.

NEWS OF DEATH

I

A pig's killed
by an experienced knife.

The simple death
of a bug in the air
is the silence, practicing.

The one watching the dying wood-pigeon
survives in a fairy-tale by Tieck.

The patient diseases
circle the body:
in its weakness it turns
light as a moth.

Gradually it burns
of an invisible light.

II

The death of a bird in the egg
will be black.

Slow death of eyes
no one looks into anymore.

Daily the dying of fingertips
while falling asleep

under the cold magnifying glass
of the moon.

Shifting sand buries
living and dead toes.

There was a massacre of voices
before silence appeared.

III

In the night, the coughing
of an unknown man.
The dark had shot
through his throat:
a black stiletto-prick.

The headless hens
run around their life
a long time,
when noon causes thirst.

The break
provided by a bottle of
bitter mineral water
is brief.
Let's take off,
as long as we hear
blood still singing in our ears.

IV

The epilsepsy of moments,
before it's a relief
to be quiet again.

The zenith puts shadows
against the wall.
They break to their knees
without a sound.

In the sky
the battle of light
when it turns afternoon.
Evening gathers in
the helpless hours.

Under the earth
the dead die one more time.

JULY AND AUGUST

July and August are like this:
the thicket
turns into a bush in heat
and the woods aren't silent either,
there's a deadly crackling. And
alternatively, things grow in cool places
where it's completely dark, nicely moist
in the momentary stillness.
It's not the right kind.
Because wet earth is silent,
where something or other rusts
away but only if you
don't put your hand there.
Suddenly, something runs off
and you don't know what it is:
a tiny bit of gauze,
alive.
And July and August remain overhead,
way up over the crowns of trees,
with jet streams as cirrus
everywhere on the horizon
and organisms moaning
beside you
that are fecund
and die.

LANDSCAPE AFTER MY HEART

A landscape after my heart,
without Baedecker's objectivity.
It only exists when I
hear myself tell things.
Air the color of Pernod
is too French, and
green gone wild resembles
the German heart in 1800.
Travel guides maintain a feeling
for substantial footwear
and the moment of awnings.
Woods in tales don't die
as long as there's breath.
I climb on through
the snow, up buried steps
in Oslo. Torches were burning
in the whiteness. There's
a lighter flaring.
When I closed my eyes
flowers were thrown after me
at night, I was pursued
by a fierce, slow-moving
full moon and
between my head and feet, my heart
beat differently.
They're not scattering blossoms
over me anymore.
My blood was hot as oil.
Now my veins are swelling
more and more.
My landscapes are roped veins,
the Scandanavian snow-torch

long since extinguished.
I'm dancing in a dream
no longer under water.
I can see bare fruit
trees clearly, with their
too-thin shadows.
But I won't get around
to saying spring anymore.
Thanks so much
for yesterday's photos.
I'm not heartless.
My way of writing grows
more casual every day.

AT DAYBREAK

Moon, mowed by the morning.

Light with its
blue scarf on our lids.

There was never so much sky
under our open shirts!
Sky, like the chest
of a man.

Bird cries
in every throat.

A time for the dead,
in order to forget death
at the window.

UNPREPARED

Without thinking I leave
the house. I lack what others
know in their bones: how we grow old,
childhood was one thing or another—
those are lost words for me.
It's good walking along in shabby clothes.
I want to hang on to my body
when I sink among people
who don't know me, I'm so sleepy, just
a guest for lunch who talks to himself
in a place that doesn't mean much.
Lost is lost. I saw you
the last time blinded by a street lamp
or waving after me.
What we're used to was abolished.
Nobody stopped when we parted.

FAMILY TABLE

The family table creates
the illusion of family.
There are empty places
everywhere.
Add father and mother
in your mind,
their forks rusty, three-tined,
a broken cup
and handy red wine spots
that grow larger
every evening.
A backdoor's open.
Someone's sneaking off.

Three

Someone Who Was Up for Anything

UNIVERSAL POEM

This is universally possible:
the picture of a woman
springing up in a man's head.
At which point she exists—
a nest of statement-sentences.
Not a secret you didn't
know before.
The answers are expected.
The night's somatic—a story
in which you hold yourself
by the hands, finally go to sleep.
It leaves
no news behind for others.
You were this air.
I won't betray it.
You found someone
who was up for anything.
Afterward, separate bodies
for separate life
which is universally possible.

COURSE OF A DAY

Witnessing the birthday of a few trees
on a morning.
I know physics is true.
Later the wind blows
over lunch tables
forgotten artworks
for metabolism.
The surface of my hand
lies in light.
That's sufficient
for the rest of the day
which clarifies everything
that follows—
a woman breathes
over my body.
I know my name
with absolute certainty,
while she makes of it
the name of an animal.

RAIN

It's like rain outside.
Nights you can be
at her side
and think of something.
A gentle machine—rain.
You can hear the cars like ships
in the odd life outside
and let your pocket knife rust
by the window, because you
won't use it after all,
with your death certificate already
in your suit pocket.
It's like rain outside.
You won't do it.
Nights you can be
at her side.
Your body's gone on.
You can fall asleep.
You won't lunge.
A gentle machine—rain.
People separate before an accident
really would have been pleasant.

LULLABY

Sleep now or at
least pretend to.
Our worldly room
grows cold as your wrist,
like skin on skin
in the cold, coming on
like winter or what we
take for it, down our hips.
Sleep now, I'll make
cold what felt different
to you—love.
My fingers in your
shoulder hair, or where
ever they get to in this
cold song.

ENTIRELY SELF-EVIDENTLY

You can make yourself your own snowman
when it's snowed,
your own sandman for the evening
for fear of loneliness and sexual intercourse.
You can say, MY FIRE
and light the rum in a cup
when you've had enough of drinking,
can do everything slowly, whatever you like
at the right time, write
and let others write, sit there
and watch women go by,
there for others,
in the right light, not
look poorly when there's blue sky
that keeps everything
going around you, presents
you—entirely self-evidently—with
whatever you weren't thinking about.

STRANGER'S HAND IN YOUR POCKET

These days lights come on earlier
everywhere in the dark.
But the time's too short to see
you, that white of your eye.
Love's like breath in the air
at a mouth opened by astonishment.
I feel your hand in my pocket.
It's warm, warms
my second Life.
The mouth's talking slowly to
itself about love. Is that the way
it really talks about everything that's
totally, wholly unreal—in that place
with the little light, a lot of darkness
everywhere—that makes you cold, throws
fog, nuts and chestnuts at you from behind?
Yes, unreal; the last light
sewed shut by the spiders.

THE END OF SOME THINGS

No one comes through the half
open door. Air moving
perhaps and the noise
of cars driving off.
Each house is just what
takes place there.
You didn't want it any other way—
making excuses
or not washing for days,
all of that a step backwards
as well as confirming obsession.
You say anything? She let
her finger trace
a run in her stocking.
You can't recognize
the end of some things.
You can't see so readily
what you've brought about.

DON'T THINK

Don't think fun's a laughing matter
and the corpses of the young are different
from the corpses of the famous that one recognizes.
With either, you have to
walk to the open window.
Places of love have other color
and odor. That varies.
Blood and sweat, they're
everywhere life is.
Terrified, naked afoot,
some rise on their toes
and listen. Nothing's up.
No roaring of leaves or waterfalls.
Earnest Time of Clear Needs
makes for lovers and corpses.
Look at both
if you have a chance.
Lust cries out briefly,
and each breath comes to an end at last.
People say, now and then:
God wants it that way.

THE OTHER SIDE

People go past, dressed, their blood
runs up their faces, so red, hypertonic.
Life, history, blood pressure—I'm not sure
whether I died last night or
a long time ago, over and over.

A hired hand, long dead, addresses me.
It's like that on the other side. No more tickets
to the lush roses. The sky stitched by swallows
was never quite right, and the homophile
lad sitting opposite tries to change my mind.
He's like a certain girl: Thanks, and that's enough now.

It's this longing to sleep, this being dead,
everything over and done, I mean everything
under your eyelids, finally freed of your senses,
or nonsense, inside and out.
No one's travelling through our tiny little land anymore,
I mean: there's really nothing in your head anymore
the way there was when I saw her the first time and
was quite dead. But I could still tell:
Love's a girl in a summer dress,
from an unread novel—how pleasant, a feeling!

I don't need room anymore for working on
living anymore, a quick glance between bushes
under the window, with night in them now.
Total deadness is quite without feeling.
A cigarette butt glows—enough of a conclusion.

THE ORDER OF THINGS

The order of things: they existed.
It's hot now. Your shirt's wet through and through.
Do away with it. You give yourself up
to me and the wind

combs us; it doesn't cool us
at twilight, or at night,
which waylays us, makes us blind
and in which we feel nothing

but force and wrists
one can press. Come, cross
your arms behind your neck, blindly.

Tear your eyes open or lower
them in the dark. We see nothing. I think
nothing now, your breath at my neck.

FINGERS

You wear your fate
on the ring finger.
Christian marriage isn't
just a sacrament,
I mean, this is
your life, friend.
The middle finger's
not going to fall off.
The ring finger's
finely articulated.
Which of the five
on the right hand's
good for firing
the gun?
Sorry, there's
no choice here either.

DEATH AS SNOWMAN

When some nice snow falls, the fever
accompanied by that deep fear rises
in my head, and I twist my coat button,
because the snow grows dearer and dearer.

And I'm snowed in and stared at
as if I were a gentle snowman.
People passing say hello in good spirits,
think of some ghost made of white earth.

Stuffed with snow, life here begins
for the first time. Good spirits grow important
the more we approach a sure end of things.

I'll be quiet as I melt to nothing.
Some nice rain will water my death,
and that deep fear will disappear just like that.

THE MURDERER

A pocketknife's enough
to kill the air
with its flying hair
and the memory of all names
left behind in it
innocently.

Just stab. You'll hit
the wind in the neck.
As dust it'll fall
at your feet.

You lift your arm.
Immediately you're
going to be
the murderer of your own breath.

AIR-CONDITIONING

Typical: a film of dust
over things:
when you turn around,
the air's already different.
It drizzles as dust
along your naked back.
The air-conditioning
looks after everything.
That paranoid feeling of fear
is there for a moment,
ineffable
in a physical world
with its telephonic commands.
Ah, ah, some whispers, wireless,
a groan from the wireless distance.
It's an appropriate call
for soul-lovers
as they write with their fingers
in the dust of their rooms:
answer me from
heaven
in an endless sentence.

CICADA

Mental: I mean, the cicada
still singing in your head
or thinks better of it now
and stops—for grace or
disgrace before your head,
which you still don't like.
Mental: the cicada sings its
way to death: come, load up,
get it through: for grace or
disgrace before your head.

MOTIVES

I

You really ought
to know about motives—
I can't say
how it came to attachment,
to inexplicable actions.
Tristan's madness
has its story
like determination and freedom.
For reasons
some plants have
leaves that constantly change.
My eyes closed,
I find my way
through the shapeless night.
I wonder how come
the end's beyond question,
while we live body to body?
I don't understand
giving every object
a different name.
Monosyllabic words
with endless meaning.
Not until your death hour
will all of that
not affect you anymore.

II

Getting
to the bottom of events

as if you were
dealing with water
you could reach through
till you drown.
A certain spirit
drives our bodies
against the earth.
Your heart beats regularly:
get out of the way
of your future.
Useless discussions
about things that
want to be alone.
Some things we get
gratis, like luck
or a cancer, the speed
hair and nails grow with.
You can't hide that
under a bushel.
Its beam strikes
an empty wall.

III

Motives that
enter the books as credit—
I'll do or not do.
The day has outlines
that correspond to my imagination:
light on skin surfaces.
Want that? Yes I do—
letting spoken words
become visible
in the cold air,
because it's winter,
follow inspiration
or, as prescribed,

be present as someone
who can make it without tears.
They say different life-systems
are a form of intelligence.
I don't want to track down
the root of my sadness.
I don't want to know
why I don't have any tears.

IV

I'm not arranging anything anymore,
because I promise myself
fewer and fewer consequences.
For no reason branches blossom
on the plane-trees
the bulldozer's torn up.
Sperm does have
something to do with love,
death's fraction everywhere between.
One should pay attention
to suppositions more often.
The yearly fall season
doesn't fall over unexpectedly
like some sort of fruit basket
when it's time.
I watch causes,
the way they develop
under my hands, unintentionally,
as touch and shivering.

SOME THINGS

There are some things
you can't do anything about.
An artery bursts, and
you watch how one
half a face changes color.
Perception's
a pursing of the mouth:
it was chewing bitter cherries
and puckered.
You thought it was meant for you.
Aversion or assent
are sometimes indistinguishable.
You go along softly
through the moving grass, crush
Damascus plums—
a special sort of fruit,
people tell you.
Chance puts a melody
in your head, without words—
forgotten
like some things
that loved you
but wouldn't say.

WHEN IT WAS TIME

When it was time
and a few night doves clucked
"dream, dream," or
something even more lovely
fell from the sky,
you stopped thinking:
That's how poems
stupefy you and no one
can keep his eyes open,
starts repeating the words
when he nods off.
Even long ago they couldn't
tell the difference between
'just one more' or 'last dance':
a verse, bleeding inside.
In the morning,
when it was time,
everything faced forward
more joyous than before.
The doves still crowded
around, didn't know who
they were anymore, and the roosters
crowed suitably,
the way you'd want them to,
mornings, in your electronic alarm.

ALL THE SAME

It's really all the same:
what day's today?
You collect greeting cards
and have no sense of time that
goes by mindlessly, wholly without you,
with your right hand writing
and your left in your pocket.
It's really all the same.
Dozing with a woman, you don't
give up, a woman who's depressed
just like you, with a fear
of everything, don't give up on
the place that's held you so long.
You can't help it,
remain and see
yourself as someone who
tears the page from the calendar
too soon, paralyzed to your eyes,
frozen to the bottom
of life that's taking
leave of him like this.

A FEEBLE AFFAIR

A feeble affair like
these difficult connections
between spring and fancy.
A body with its cancer
can still be beautiful for a while
before it gets its death.
We fight sickness,
call it emancipated life.
A bit of self-confidence suffices—
sleeping in wet clothes
after making love that smelled so good,
bird cries, and red wine in your throat.
Later old age, it's flat.
Tell about it when you get there.
A body, with its
deadly infection, grows light.
It'll sleep
to its end.

THE YEAR

They say birds
sing themselves to death.
Spring's difficult,
because the sky's
three times as beautiful.
People play with life
and don't know it.
On a summer night
a man's got to have
a sweetheart,
Kleist says in Thun.
The Kleist
Robert Walser
invented on his journeys.
The grass isn't
growing any higher,
and God's round
in summer: a ball of light.
Later you freeze
between the shoulder blades,
don't want to believe it.
There's leaffall this time too,
and what follows.
It's not cold yet,
but free-time outside's
getting tiny.
And in the dark,
pious November weeks
they're playing soccer.
You look for a handkerchief
and find your soul.
That's not quite right.
The year's over,
the calendar says so.

LIFE

for Siegfried Unseld

Between loving and no longer loving
ashes fall from the air.
The ones who've stayed away a long time
exist as fragrance, not as shadow.

The ones who don't return
lose themselves from night to night.
Whatever makes you bitter or sweet
was devoured by life.

THE HOUSE THAT HOLDS EVERYTHING

The house that holds everything—
its furniture avoids me.
No wind's asleep behind the walls.
I put my foot to the floor.
I try locked doors
and dream the long dream
of a brief survival.
I sense: the lights
going on in my town.
Nobody there for me.
I'm holding the hand
of someone, in this dream, due to fear,
to hate or love, to coincidence.
As long as I can look
for another face . . .
Outside, all the lights
are on everywhere now.
Shining bulbs from the years
when room after room grew
from the house that holds everything
and nothing from the rest of the world.

STAYING ALIVE

We insist on
staying alive,
count on ten fingers
what we take for luck,
look into various faces,
get helloed, say hello back,
experience physical maturity.
Light falls in a straight line
when it's noon and
the emotions are subdued.
I don't run after words anymore
when I sleep right next to you
and don't notice how fast
we fail and go silent.

YEARS UPON YEARS

You know, I'm not good
for much. I don't want
to seem familiar, I'd rather
not name the right
examples. I stand
around shyly in spring.
The grass comes up like hair growing.
Each season just imitates
itself you know. Summer's
crazy, with its round sun.
Storms keep away and
the applesauce will be
as spoiled by August
as it is the next time.
Half the night's begun.
The church hymn astonishes me.
I sing along and choke:
yesterday my voice
hadn't changed yet.
I take up with the cold
and freeze, so that's eternity!
Years upon years.
Men attend to women.
Women are different. My naiveté
is unstoppable. Hosannah.
I try hard in the usual ways.
I have to get along with
whatever you entrust to me.
You know, I'm really
not good for much.

THE SKIN YOU'RE STUCK IN

The mechanical toy of my childhood,
imagination, aged by now,
earlier a means of not being seen.
Lamp and cabinet tell me
I live somewhere, without possessing me.
You get used to the skin
you're stuck in.
Reality—a succession of images
driven by selection.
Inbetween: sleep, lying next to each other,
the approach of death.
She wore some dress or other
her legs and thighs showed through.
Forget everything. The approach
of some devastation or other.
What'll we do with this life?